W9-BNR-894

Birds up close

RAPTORS

A Bobbie Kalman Book

Crabtree Publishing Company

Birds up close
A Bobbie Kalman Book

For Stacey and in memory of Olive

Editor-in-Chief
Bobbie Kalman

Writing team
Bobbie Kalman
Jacqueline Langille
Niki Walker

Managing editor
Lynda Hale

Series editor
Niki Walker

Editor
Greg Nickles

Text and photo research
Jacqueline Langille

Computer design
Lynda Hale
Andy Gecse (cover concept)

Production coordinator
Hannelore Sotzek

Photographs
Grady Harrison: page 18
Robert J. Huffman/Field Mark Publications: pages 20, 21
James Kamstra: pages 12, 19, 26, 27 (right top and bottom)
Rick Kline/Cornell Laboratory of Ornithology: page 11 (top)
Robert McCaw: pages 10, 11 (bottom), 13, 17, 31 (bottom)
Sylvia Stevens: pages 27(left), 28
Dave Taylor: pages 5 (top), 9 (top), 22, 29
Tom Stack & Associates: Mark Newman: page 16; Roy Toft: page 30
Valan Photos/Rob Simpson: page 31 (top)
Jerry Whitaker: page 23
Other photographs by Digital Vision and Digital Stock

Illustrations
Doug Swinamer: pages 15, 18

Consultant
Ron Rohrbaugh, Cornell
Laboratory of Ornithology

Color separations and film
Dot 'n Line Image Inc.

Printer
Worzalla Publishing Company

Crabtree Publishing Company

350 Fifth Avenue	360 York Road, RR 4,	73 Lime Walk
Suite 3308	Niagara-on-the-Lake,	Headington
New York	Ontario, Canada	Oxford OX3 7AD
N.Y. 10118	L0S 1J0	United Kingdom

Copyright © **1998 CRABTREE PUBLISHING COMPANY**.
All rights reserved. No part of this publication may be
reproduced, stored in a retrieval system or be transmitted
in any form or by any means, electronic, mechanical,
photocopying, recording, or otherwise, without the prior
written permission of Crabtree Publishing Company.

Cataloging in Publication Data
Kalman, Bobbie
  Raptors
(Birds up close)
Includes index.
ISBN 0-86505-751-6 (library bound)   ISBN 0-86505-765-6 (pbk.)
This book introduces the body adaptations, predatory behavior, and
breeding of raptors, or birds of prey, including the osprey, bald eagle,
owls, and falcons.

1. Birds of prey—Juvenile literature. [1. Birds of prey] I. Title. II. Series:
Kalman, Bobbie. Birds up close.

QL696.F3K35 1997   j598.9   LC 97-39893
                                                         CIP

Contents

What are raptors?

Raptors are birds of prey. Birds of prey catch other animals for food. Many birds eat other animals, but they catch their food with their beak. Raptors are the only birds that almost always catch their prey with their feet.

Raptors of all kinds

There are more than 450 types of raptors. They are grouped into families of eagles, kites, hawks, falcons, vultures, and owls. Two special types of raptors —the osprey and the secretary bird—have only one species in each family.

Different types of eagles are found all over the world. The two in this picture are African fish eagles. They live near lakes, rivers, and other inland bodies of water.

Around the world

Raptors live all over the world, except on Antarctica. They live in almost every type of **habitat**, from thick rainforest to dry grassland. A habitat is a place in nature where an animal makes its home. Some raptors, such as peregrine falcons, even live in cities!

(*above*) *Instead of hunting prey, some raptors such as vultures eat mostly dead animals that they find on the ground.*

(*left*) *Most raptors hunt in the daytime, but many owls hunt at night. They are* **nocturnal***.*

In the photograph above, the jackal buzzard's feet are poised to grab prey. Raptors are excellent hunters and hardly ever miss their target. If they do miss, they fly up and try again.

Catching prey

Some raptors such as falcons attack their prey from the sky. They fly around looking for an animal and then dive toward it. At the last moment, they swing out their feet and grab the prey with their talons. Other raptors such as owls perch on a tree branch to wait for prey.

Sky divers

Eagles, hawks, and falcons fly high above the ground to watch for prey. They fly over fields and other open areas and dive quickly to catch a mouse or rabbit before it can run away. Ospreys and some eagles fly over lakes and streams to look for fish. They dive and grab fish right out of the water.

Snake stalkers

Secretary birds walk quietly through savannahs to hunt for snakes. They listen carefully to hear a snake slithering in the grass. When they find a snake, they stomp on its head to kill it.

Snakes are very quiet, but secretary birds have great hearing.

Ospreys eat mostly fish. When they catch a fish, they fly to a nearby perch to eat it.

Eating prey

Raptors eat many types of food. Some small raptors hunt mostly insects. Larger raptors, such as the great horned owl shown opposite, eat larger prey. This owl has almost no sense of smell. It is one of the few animals that can eat skunks!

Water from fresh food

Raptors do not need to drink water as often as other birds do. They get some water from the animals they eat. When raptors do drink, they scoop water into their lower beak and tip their head back to let the water run down their throat.

Raptors try to protect their meal from the other birds of prey that would steal it. This goshawk is **mantling***, or spreading its wings, to hide its prey.*

Unchewed food

Many raptors swallow their prey whole or in chunks. Their body uses the meat, but it cannot digest the bones and teeth. Raptors cough up a ball of bones and teeth wrapped in feathers or fur. It is called a **pellet**. Scientists study pellets to find out what raptors eat. A pile of pellets below a tree means that tree is a favorite raptor perch.

Pairing and raising young

To make eggs, most birds find breeding partners, or **mates**, once each year. The male and female work together to raise their young. Most male raptors have only one female partner a year. Larger raptors often have the same mate for life. Some males have to win a new mate every year.

Raising their young

Young raptors are very weak when they hatch. Their parents bring prey to the nest and tear off pieces for them to eat. When they are older, they watch their parents hunt. Young raptors must wait for their flight feathers to grow before they can leave the nest and learn to hunt.

As soon as they can fly, chicks begin to grab food from their parents' talons in midair. They are able to hunt on their own before long. This golden eagle chick still has too much down to fly away from the nest. Some raptors wait more than two months for their flight feathers.

Courting a mate

To win a mate, a male sometimes brings a gift of food to a female to show her that he is a good hunter. Showing off to win a mate is called **courting**. Male raptors also show off their flying skills to attract a female. Some males fly very fast or very high. Others dive and swoop. Fancy flying to attract a mate is a type of **courtship display**.

Building a nest

Most raptors build a nest to hold their eggs. Eagle and falcon nests are called **eyries**. Raptors often build their nest high in a tree. They use branches, twigs, and grasses. Some raptors lay their eggs on cliff ledges or in a hole in a tree.

(opposite) Young raptor chicks pull pieces of meat out of their parent's beak. When they get older, they tear apart the meat themselves.

Eagles and hawks

Eagles and hawks belong to a group of raptors called **accipitrids**. They are well known for their flying abilities. Eagles are larger than hawks, but there are not many other differences between these birds. Kites and harriers are also accipitrids. Many of these birds use their sharp talons to kill prey.

Sneak attacks

When hunting, many accipitrids use their flying skills to sneak up on prey. Some hawks fly close to the ground behind a hedge or fence. They swoop quickly over the hedge into the middle of a flock of small birds. The small birds have very little time to escape.

Other accipitrids hide in trees and use surprise attacks to catch their prey. When they see a small animal below their tree, they dive to the ground and grab it.

More about eagles and hawks

Different types: 210 species
Length: 4 - 48 inches (10 - 122 cm)
Weight: 4 ounces - 14½ pounds (113 g - 6.6 kg)
Food: Mammals, birds, fish, amphibians, reptiles, and insects

Sky-dancing

During the mating season, eagles and hawks make fantastic courtship displays. Some eagles lock talons in midair, spin around, and tumble toward the ground. Harriers practice **sky-dancing**. They climb and dive, up and down, over and over. Sky-dancing can last for many minutes and cover great distances.

The bald eagle

Less than 30 years ago, the bald eagle was in danger of disappearing forever, or becoming **extinct**. People killed thousands of bald eagles with guns and traps. Many more were poisoned by a chemical called DDT, which people sprayed to kill mosquitoes.

Rain washed the DDT into lakes and rivers, poisoning the fish. Many bald eagles were poisoned when they ate the fish. These bald eagles began laying eggs with thin shells, which were crushed when the birds sat on them. Fewer and fewer baby bald eagles hatched.

Saving a raptor

After 1952, people were no longer allowed to hunt the bald eagle, and in 1972, they stopped spraying DDT. By that time, almost all the bald eagles were gone.

To increase the bird's population, scientists began a captive breeding program. They hatched bald eagle eggs and raised the chicks themselves. When the bald eagle chicks grew up, they were taken to a wilderness area and released.

Back from the brink

The bald eagle has slowly returned from the edge of extinction. Many of these raptors now live in the wilderness areas of North America. Every fall, a large group of bald eagles gathers on the Chilkat River in Alaska to catch salmon. As many as 4,000 birds stay in one ten-mile (16 km) section of the riverbank.

(opposite) The bald eagle is now protected by law, and its numbers are slowly increasing. Today, at least 80,000 bald eagles live in North America.

? More about bald eagles

Length: Up to 3 feet (0.9 m)

Weight: $4^{1}/_{2}$ - 13 pounds (2 - 6 kg)

Wingspan: 6 - 7 feet (3 m) from tip to tip when fully spread

Food: Mainly fish; also water birds and small mammals

Nest: World's largest tree nest—up to $9^{1}/_{2}$ feet (2.9 m) wide and 20 feet (6 m) deep; built from sticks and twigs and added onto year after year

Eggs: 2 - 3, white to pale blue

Brooding: 35 days; parents take turns sitting on the eggs

Falcons

Falcons resemble eagles and hawks, but they do not belong to the same family. Falcons, falconets, and caracaras belong to the falcon family. Unlike other raptors, these birds kill their prey with their beak. They catch prey with their feet and bite it on the neck. Most falcons eat smaller birds that they catch in flight.

Many falcons perch on branches or posts to look for prey. A falcon bobs its head up and down when it sees something move. This movement helps the bird focus its eyes on the moving target. When the falcon's eyes focus, the bird can tell how far away the prey is. The bird then knows how far and fast to fly to catch it.

Caracaras bend over backwards to call to each other. Some people think they are named after their strange, rattling call.

(opposite) American kestrels nest in tree holes. They balance against the trunk with their tail.

Tomial teeth

A few types of falcons are the only raptors that have a notch, or "tooth," on each side of their upper beak. These notches are called **tomial teeth**. Scientists think these teeth help falcons quickly kill their prey. Tomial teeth hold the prey in the sharp front part of the falcon's beak.

More about falcons

Different types: 61 species;
    smallest: African pygmy falcon;
    largest: gyrfalcon
Length: 5 - 24 inches (13 - 61 cm)
Weight: 1$\frac{1}{2}$ ounces - 4$\frac{1}{2}$ pounds
    (43 g - 2 kg)
Food: birds, insects, lizards, snakes,
    and mammals

Training raptors

For more than 2,000 years, people have trained raptors to catch food for them. Training a raptor is called **falconry** or **hawking**. The birds are trained to kill and bring back prey or wait with it until the **falconer**, or trainer, comes to get it.

New ways of hunting

People almost gave up falconry when guns were invented. With guns, hunters could easily shoot their own prey. Some hunters began to think hawks were eating too much prey, so they started shooting hawks to get rid of them.

Falconry today

Today, falconry is practiced around the world as a pastime. The peregrine falcon is a favorite raptor for falconry. Hawks and some eagles are also trained. Each raptor is best at hunting a certain type of prey in a certain area. For example, peregrine falcons catch birds in open spaces such as fields and meadows. Other raptors are suited to hunting birds and small mammals in areas covered with trees or bushes.

(opposite) The raptor perches on its trainer's hand before it flies out to hunt. Falconers wear a thick leather glove to protect their hand from the raptor's sharp talons.

Raptors on the job

Small birds sometimes crash into airplanes as they take off and land. People have trained some raptors to scare other birds away from runways. Raptors are also trained to keep small birds from eating the fruit growing on farms.

(above) Falconry hoods keep birds calm. A falcon stays quiet under its hood and does not get excited by activity around it.

Only the osprey

One of the few raptors that is found all over the world is the osprey. Ospreys eat mostly fish and live near the water on seacoasts, rivers, and lakes.

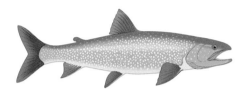

Ospreys have special joints in their wings to help them fish. Their wings bend almost backwards in the middle. Bending their wings helps ospreys fly up out of the water after they dive in for a fish.

? More about ospreys

Length: 22 - 24 inches (56 - 61 cm)
Weight: 2½ - 4 pounds (1 - 2 kg)
Food: Mainly fish; some birds and sea snakes
Nest: Built of sticks and grasses, often in trees or on cliffs, with a view of the water
Eggs: 2 - 4, creamy-white blotched with brown
Brooding: Female broods about 35 days

Expert fishers

Ospreys catch a fish almost every time they try. They dive down to the water and catch fish swimming near the surface. An osprey holds onto slippery fish with **spinules** on the bottom of its feet. The short, sharp spinules work with its talons to grip the slimy fish firmly.

Reversible toes

Special toes also help ospreys grab and carry their prey. They can turn their outer toes completely to the back so that two toes face backward and two toes face forward. Reversing their toes gives ospreys a stronger grip. Ospreys and owls are the only raptors that have these **reversible toes**.

The secretary bird

Secretary birds are the only raptors with long legs. Unlike other raptors, which hunt from the air, these birds hunt on the ground. Their long legs help them walk among tall grasses and run after fast prey.

Walking and stalking

Each morning, the secretary bird jumps down from its perch and starts hunting. To scare small animals out of the grass, the bird stamps its feet on the ground. It runs quickly after a mouse or lizard and catches the prey with its beak.

Snake killers

The secretary bird also preys on poisonous snakes. The bird's legs and thick wing feathers protect it from snakebites. The legs are covered with tough scales that a snake's fangs cannot pierce. The thick feathers on the bird's wings also prevent fangs from reaching its skin and poisoning the bird. To kill a snake, the secretary bird grabs it near its head and breaks its spine or carries the snake high in the air and drops it.

Secretary birds live in Africa. They usually live in pairs. They roost together at night in a low, thorny tree. The secretary bird is named for the long black feathers on its head. The feathers look like the quill pens secretaries used long ago.

More about secretary birds

Height: 4 feet (1.2 m)
Weight: 7 - 9 pounds (3 - 4 kg)
Food: Mice and other small animals, insects, lizards, and snakes
Nest: Large, flat nest of sticks, lined with grass, in a low thorny tree
Eggs: 2 - 3, greenish white
Brooding: Parents take turns for 45 days

Masters of midnight

Owls are the among the few types of raptors that hunt at night. About 80 species of owls are nocturnal. Others are **crepuscular**, which means they hunt in the dim light of dawn and dusk.

Finding prey

Night hunters need excellent eyesight and hearing to find prey in the dark. Most owls can see better in the dark than people can see during the day. Owls hear so well that they can find prey even when they cannot see it.

Silent flight

Owls are almost silent when they fly, so they are able to sneak up on their prey. Unlike the wings of other birds, the edges of an owl's wings have soft feathers that make no noise when they move through the air.

(left) Owl eyes point forward and do not move around much. To see more, an owl can turn its head almost in a circle.

More about owls

Different types: 133 species; smallest: elf owl; largest: eagle owl
Length: 5 - 28 inches (13 - 71 cm)
Weight: 3 ounces - 9 pounds (85 g - 4 kg)
Food: Mice, rats, squirrels, rabbits, birds, fish, crabs, insects, and spiders

(left) A barn owl eats about 1,500 mice a year. A barn owl family eats 6,000!

(top) At night, baby owls wait for their parents to bring back prey for them to eat.

(bottom) In a couple months, baby owls are almost the same size as their parents.

Carrion eaters

Vultures eat mostly **carrion**, or the meat of animals that are already dead. They have thinner and weaker talons than other raptors. They do not need strong talons for gripping because their prey never moves.

Strong stomach

Most carrion has started to rot when vultures find it. Rotten meat makes people sick, but vultures have a special stomach with strong acid that keeps them from getting sick.

Some large vultures are also known as condors. The vulture on the left is an Andean condor.

(right) Vultures often feed in large groups. This group is feeding on a large animal carcass. Most vultures have a bare head, which is easy to keep clean when the birds eat such messy food.

Too stuffed to fly

Many vultures do not eat every day. They must wait until they find a carcass. When a vulture does find food, it eats as much as possible. It gets so full that it becomes too heavy to fly. If an enemy comes near, the vulture has to throw up its meal before it can fly away!

? More about vultures

Different types: 7 New World vultures, including condors; 14 Old World vultures
Length: 24 - 50 inches (61 - 127 cm)
Weight: 2 - 28 pounds (1 - 13 kg)
Food: Carrion; sometimes small live animals, birds' eggs, and fruit

On the brink

Many raptors are killed every year. Some are shot by people because they think raptors eat farm animals. Many are hit by cars. Others die when they eat the poisoned food people put out to kill coyotes. Raptor habitats are lost when people cut down trees and replace other wilderness areas with houses, roads, and shopping malls.

One type of raptor—the California condor—is almost extinct. In 1987, there were only 27 of these birds left. A captive breeding program was started and, in 1992, scientists released two California condors into the Sespe Condor Sanctuary in California. Today a group of 20 lives in the sanctuary, and 100 California condors live in zoos.

Rehabilitation centers

People sometimes find an injured raptor before it dies. They bring it to a special place called a **rehabilitation center**, where people help raptors get better. A raptor's injuries are treated by veterinarians. When the raptor is healthy, it is returned to the wild. Some raptors do not heal properly. The people at the center take care of them for the rest of their lives.

(above) Raptors are often killed by power lines. They fly very quickly when they chase prey and do not see the wire until they fly into it.

(left) Eastern screech owls need dead trees in which to build nests. Loggers cut down many old trees, so the owls have no place to nest and raise their chicks.

(opposite) Scientists raise California condor chicks with special puppets that look like the adult bird's head and neck. When the chicks grow up, they are released into the wild.

Words to know

breed To make babies

brood To sit on eggs so they will hatch; also to sit over chicks to warm them

captive breeding Taking birds from the wild for the purpose of mating them, raising their babies, and returning them safely to the wild

carcass The body of a dead animal

courtship display A set of actions performed to attract a mate

extinct Describing a type of animal that has died out

family A group of animals with similar appearances and habits

habitat The place where a plant or animal is usually found in nature

predator An animal that kills and eats other animals

prey An animal that is hunted and eaten by another animal

raptor A bird of prey that catches its prey with its feet

talon A long, curved claw on each toe of a raptor's foot

Index

1 2 3 4 5 6 7 8 9 0   Printed in the U.S.A.   6 5 4 3 2 1 0 9 8 7